Dedicated to Michael Bixler (1946–2024)

HEBREW MONOTYPE

AT THE BIXLER PRESS & LETTERFOUNDRY

Shani Avni

Dry Inc.

3
6
9
12
15
18
21
24
27
30
33
36
39

ISBN 978-0-9631082-9-6

Hebrew Type Intensive at the Press and Letterfoundry of Michael and Winifred Bixler

The Bixler Letterfoundry in Skaneateles, New York, is one of a handful of shops in the United States that professionally preserves the legacy of typecasting and letterpress printing. For more than fifty years they have been producing newly cast metal typefaces to support educational institutions and the artistic work of fine press printers.

Specializing in limited edition letterpress books set on the Monotype typecasting system, they are honored to be part of the historic bookmaking process, where each project is experienced as a thoughtful and careful journey.[1]

Winifred "Winnie" (Gray) Bixler and Michael Bixler met in 1969 when they were students at the Rochester Institute of Technology. They married and relocated to Boston to establish their first Monotype shop in 1973. A decade later, they moved to Skaneateles and began restoring an 1867 historic brick mill building, former home of Skaneateles Handicrafters, where Marshall Larabee started a line of wooden trains and other toys for mass production.

Over the years the Bixlers focused on acquiring classic English Monotype matrices (molds for casting type) for selected Latin typefaces.[2] In addition, they collected some rare Hebrew Monotype matrices.

The Hebrew Type Intensive was launched in the last week of July 2023. The four-day workshop was designed to provide participants an immersive, hands-on experience of the historical aspects of Jewish printing: casting type, typesetting, and letterpress printing, using the Hebrew matrices from the Bixlers' collection.

Each morning opened with a lecture by Shani Avni, who introduced the history of Jewish type and typography. During the lectures the participants learned about the development of the Hebrew script and the challenging transition from its written form to movable type. The stories behind the matrices and typefaces from the Bixler collection were discussed, with emphasis on the barriers Hebrew type production has suffered and how these affect the reading experience of Jewish languages.

Starting in the afternoons and going well into the evenings, participants worked intensively. Grace Gist, the casting technician, held casting demonstrations throughout the workshop. The demonstrations included casting 14-point Peninim 220 for composition, as well as the same typeface, size 24-point, on the Display Super Caster. The participants observed the casting process and gained a deep understanding of metal type production. In addition to learning about the intricacies of casting type, the participants witnessed the various adaptations needed for casting Hebrew letters on machinery that was perfected to support Latin letters. This firsthand experience clarified why and how Hebrew type was poorly cast and printed throughout history, and specifically during the nineteenth and twentieth centuries.

Leading the letterpress-printing portion of the workshop, Richard Kegler held demonstrations and supported each participant with their personal project from concept to completion. Winifred Bixler and Seth Gottlieb provided additional guidance and support.

Coming from different backgrounds with varying levels of letterpress-printing experience, each participant planned an ambitious print of their chosen Hebrew or Yiddish text. Not shying away from dealing with additional challenges and under a strict deadline, they engaged with combining metal and wood type, setting Hebrew with Latin, using the Hebrew diacritic marks, and exploring color options. With great focus and dedication, all of them completed an impressive portfolio.

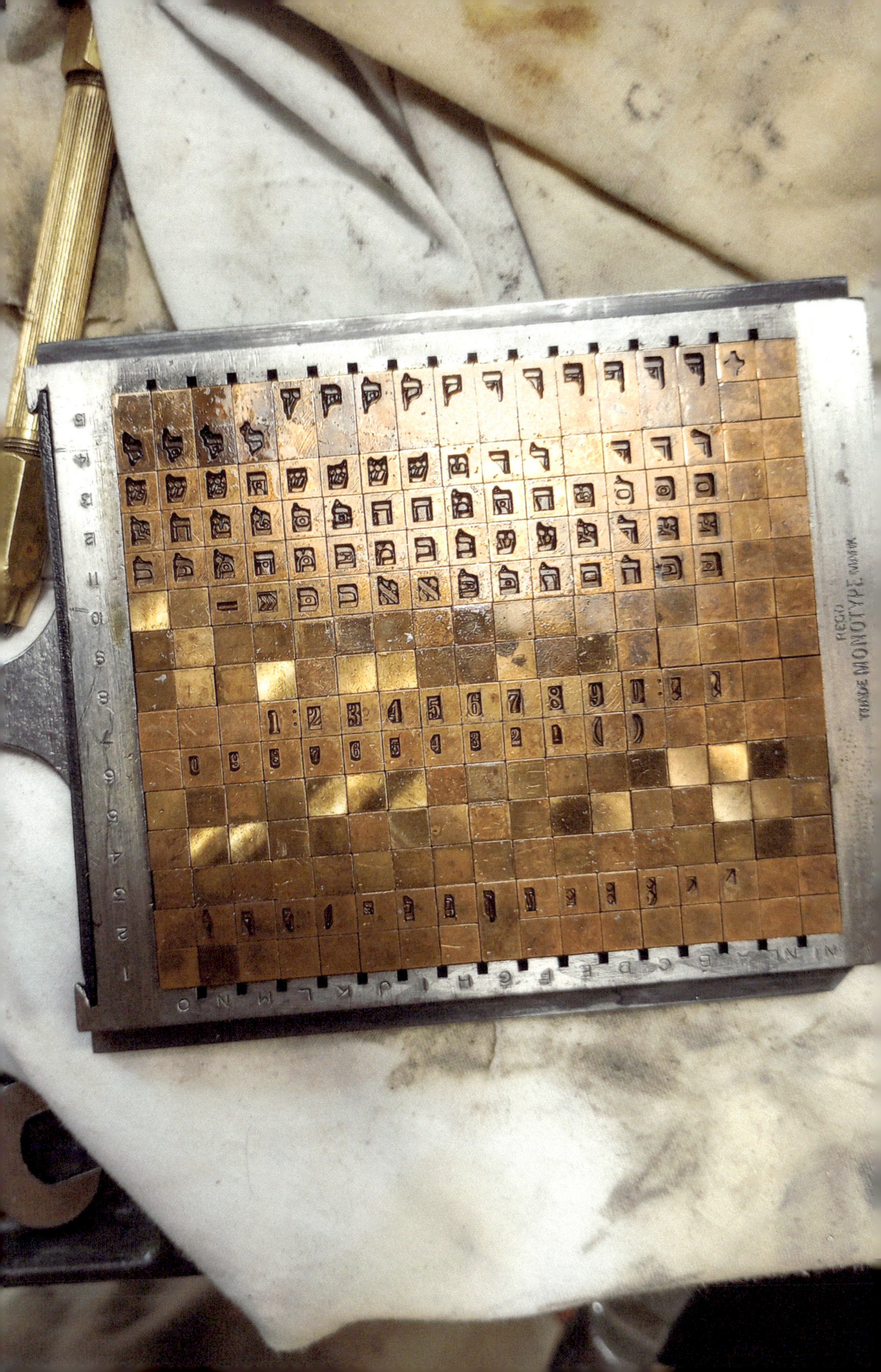

The Portfolio

Lynne Avadenka

Robyn Awend

Sophie Edelhart

Barbara Mann

Noam Sienna

Nancy Sinkoff

In addition to working with metal type, the participants used wood type that was created by Virgin Wood Type manufacturing company, of Rochester, New York. In 2023, RIT Cary Graphic Arts Collection commissioned them to produce two Hebrew fonts, based on historical original patterns from the company's collection. Geri McCormick and James Grieshaber of Virgin Wood Type visited the workshop and presented on making historic Hebrew wood type and the complexities it entails.

Hebrew Script Overview

- Hebrew is a single-case alphabetic script consisting of twenty-two letters and five additional final forms: letters that are formed differently when they appear as the last letter of a word.

- Hebrew is written from right to left and supports various Jewish languages such as Hebrew, Yiddish, and Ladino.

- Other than the consonants *aleph*, *hea*, *vav*, and *yud* that assist in indicating vocalization, the Hebrew alphabet lacks vowel letters. The vocalization system, called *niqqud*, is a set of diacritic marks added above, below, and within the characters in order to distinguish between alternative pronunciations of letters.

- Biblical text requires additional specialized marks as well as cantillation marks called *te'amim*, used as musical notation for chanting rituals.

- Modern Jewish languages use Hindu-Arabic numerals and Latin punctuation marks with the addition of the Hebrew *maqaf*. Although the punctuation marks are mostly identical to the Latin ones, their height and angle should be adapted to Hebrew.

- There is only one traditional formalized *aleph-lamed* ligature. In 1985, the *shin-het* ligature representing the Israeli currency symbol was designed by Moshe Pereg.

- Hebrew typefaces traditionally do not include typographic tools equivalent to Latin such as italics or small caps.

Hebrew Type and Typography

The development of the Hebrew script around the sixth century BCE took a unique course partly for the reason that according to Jewish tradition the Hebrew letterforms were considered to be sacred and to carry a complex religious meaning. Since the second century BCE and for centuries to come, Hebrew was mostly confined to religious use and only qualified, devout scribes were permitted, under strict rules, to write religious manuscripts. Using mostly the formal square style, the form of the letters had to be maintained and preserved, even at the cost of poor readability. As the square Hebrew style was rigidly copied, it did not evolve at the same rate as a secular script would.[3]

With the earliest dated Hebrew book printed in 1475, Hebrew printers could be considered as early adopters of Gutenberg's mechanized printing technology. As religious Hebrew manuscripts played a central role in their lives, printing them instead of copying them by hand increased the production and distribution of these texts and contributed to Hebrew readership.[4] However, movable type was mechanized based on Latin script and so the creation of Hebrew typefaces presented numerous challenges. The nature of Hebrew writing, which was one of self-production versus commercial production, meant that there were no clear unified writing models to serve as references for drawing and cutting the letters.[5]

Moreover, the Jewish communities scattered among various nations in Europe were at the mercy of the authorities' attitude toward them. They suffered repeated persecution and were often barred from printing or forced to flee and relocate their presses. Such disruption prevented the continuous natural development needed for the refinement of type. In addition, most of the professionals that were engaged with cutting type were not familiar with the nuances of the Hebrew script and introduced misinterpretations. This flawed transition from the handwritten form to the printed form led to poor quality typefaces that lost the authentic structure of the letterforms and the visual traces of the written form.

The nineteenth century marked a growing demand for printed matter in Jewish languages. Jewish communities around the world were seeking books, newspapers, periodicals, and sheet music in the Hebrew script that supported their local native tongues. Additionally, the Hebrew language was veering away from traditional religious confines and toward revival as a spoken secular language. This cultural shift was represented in the Jewish Enlightenment movement that aimed to acquaint Jews with the Hebrew language and secular education and culture as supplements to traditional religious studies. Additionally, the Zionist movement promoted a homeland for Jews in Mandatory Palestine and used Jewish languages in printed media. The demand for printed matter in Hebrew grew rapidly and the existing typefaces failed to support this increasing growth.[6]

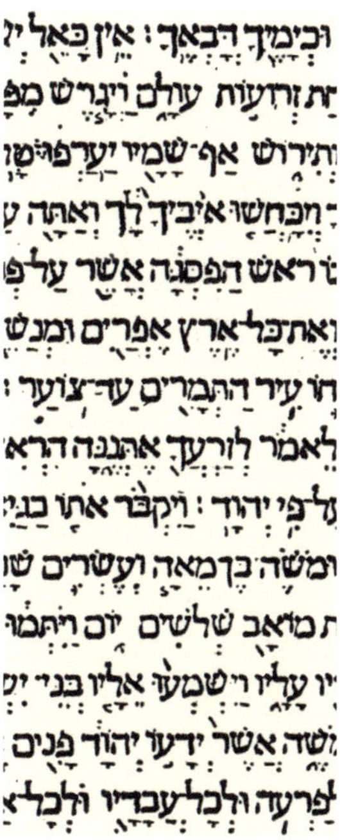

Detail of printed Hebrew from: *Soncino Bible*, Soncino, 1488.

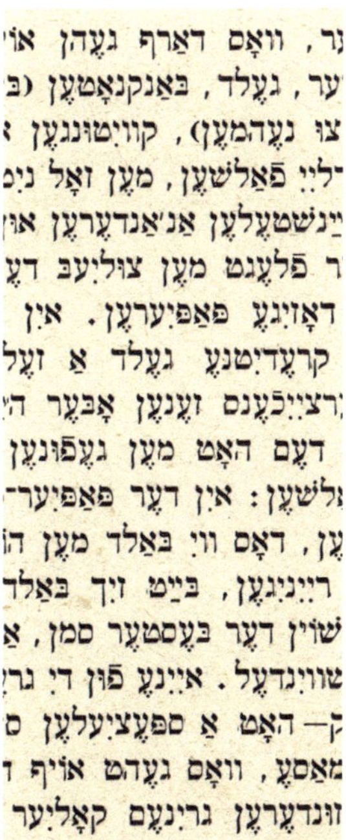

Detail of printed Yiddish from: *Zamelbukh Kultur*, Minsk: Ferlag Kultur, 1905.

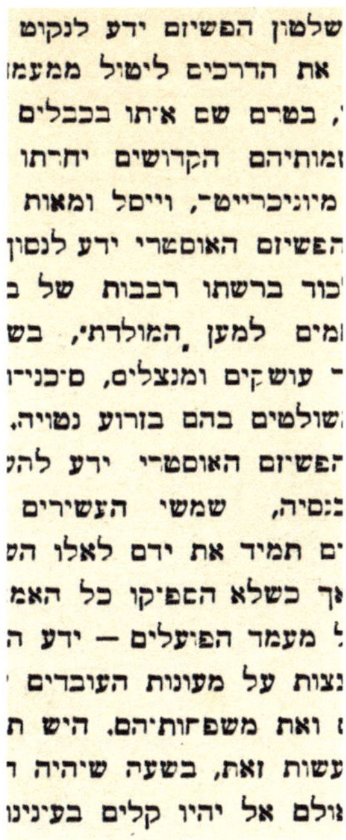

Detail of printed Hebrew from: *BaMaale* newspaper, Tel-Aviv: Achdut Press, 1935.

Hebrew Monotype in the United States

Prior to 1914, American-Jewish communities were mostly importing Hebrew books and periodicals from Germany, England, and the Netherlands. During the First World War, many European Jewish presses were destroyed and the access to Hebrew printed matter in the United States was restricted. In response, the Jewish Publication Society of America embarked on founding a Jewish press in New York City. They raised funds to acquire two European-manufactured Monotype machines with duplex keyboards, commissioned Lanston Monotype US Assistant Art Director Sol Hess to create the No. 280M Classic Hebrew typeface,[7] and established the Hebrew Monotype Press Inc. in 1921.[8]

The machines had to be modified in order to function in Hebrew. The Lanston Monotype Machine Company introduced the reverse delivery mechanism for the caster in 1910, permitting right-to-left type composition. In this setup, the sorts were pushed out upside down and backwards to accommodate the Hebrew script writing direction, then the lines had to be turned around manually one by one.[9] The Latin key-banks, key-bars, and stop-bars were substituted with keys bearing the Hebrew characters. Since the matrix of each character was placed in the matrix case upside down, the nick was created at the top of each sort, instead of the bottom.[10]

Prior to mechanical composition, casting and setting the niqqud was highly time consuming and costly, leading publishers to produce unvocalized books and periodicals, under the assumption that readers would be able to decipher words according to their context.[11] In the instances that Hebrew typefaces for hand-composition were produced with the full character sets to include the niqqud, the letters were cut once without any marks, and again with specific marks, each representing a different pronunciation. The niqqud marks were also cast individually and hand-set below or above the characters accordingly.[12]

Holam Haser [o] Hiriq [i] Dagesh [b,k,p]

Examples of three niqqud marks placed above, below, and within the character. The placement distinguishes between alternative pronunciation of certain letters.

Mechanical composition emerged in the nineteenth century with the Linotype machine's novelty of producing solid "lines of type." The disadvantage was that in the event of a typographic error, the entire line had to be broken up and recomposed, introducing the risk of new errors.[13]

It appears that early Hebrew Linotype typefaces excluded the niqqud altogether due to its technical complexity.[14] However, it became available in some capacity at a later time, as indicated in undated Linotype specimens of the typeface Pointed Hebrew which was possibly used to print vocalized Israeli newspapers intended for people learning Hebrew.[15]

The letter aleph without niqqud, next to an aleph with the niqqud mark *kamatz*, and an aleph with the niqqud mark *patach* cast as single sorts in 24-point Peninim 220.

The Monotype mechanism offered significant improvement with the ability to cast individual letters, which were assembled into lines, allowing more flexibility in the typesetting process. The width of the widest character was divided into eighteen units, and the rest of the characters were derived from it, with the narrowest being five units. For most Hebrew Monotype typefaces, only two widths were afforded. With this mechanism it was possible to effectively replicate the niqqud hand-typesetting approach. Having each niqqud mark in two width sizes, usually 9 units and 18 units, allowed the keyboard operator to synchronize the narrow letters with the narrow marks and the wide letters with the wide marks and correctly match either vowels or spaces of equal widths to the characters in the previous lines above.[16]

Monotype's Impact on Hebrew Type Design

The introduction of the Hebrew Monotype was met with great enthusiasm as it provided necessary opportunities for Jewish printing.[17] However, the restrictions of mechanical composition resulted in various deformities to the authentic Hebrew letterform structures: as characters were either stretched or condensed in order to fit into limited specific widths, their original proportions were significantly altered.

Additionally, the inclusion of the niqqud meant that the comprehensive character set was downsized in order to fit within the existing matrix case. Therefore, the less frequently used characters were omitted and not produced. These were alternative calligraphic letterforms traditionally used to improve and enrich Hebrew texts: the aleph-lamed ligature, as well as wide versions of several letters that were used for block alignment.[18] These characters made their way into some early printing type but did not survive technological advancements. Subsequently, they disappeared from printed matter, most probably only to resurface at the age of digital type technology.

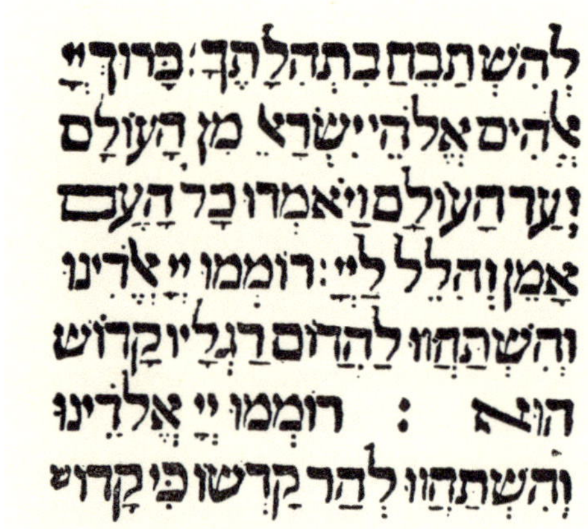
להשתבח בתהלתך: ברוך יי
אלהים אלהי ישרא' מן העולם
ועד העולם ויאמרו כל העם
אמן והלל ליי: רוממו יי אלהינו
והשתחוו להדום רגליו קדוש
הוא : רוממו יי אלהינו
והשתחוו להר קדשו כי קדוש

Examples of an incunabula font printed in Spain with the aleph-lamed ligature (second and fourth line) and wide versions of the letters final mem and aleph (third and sixth line).

Fragment. [Hispania]. Ordo precum. B 43. Freimann, Aron and Marx, Moses. *Thesaurus Typographiae Hebraicae Saeculi* XV. Berlin-Wilmersdorf: Universitas-Booksellers, 1924–1931.

Moreover, with only one character with an ascender and a small number of characters with descenders, the effort of casting these characters on larger type bodies was probably impractical. The lack of backing for these overhanging strokes very often led to them breaking. As resources were usually costly and time consuming, typesetters used the broken characters resulting in poor printing that ultimately damaged the readability and legibility of printed text.

Finally, it seems that experienced Hebrew type designers were not involved in most Hebrew Monotype production processes. In the event they were, their requested corrections were not realized due to unfeasible costs, technical constraints, and the extensive time frame required for implementation.[19]

During the process of casting the 24-point Peninim 220 letter lamed, a larger point size and modified matrix holder were used in order to support the ascender and minimize the overhang that would tend to break.

During the late 1950s the Monotype corporation started to raise concerns regarding future production of additional Hebrew typefaces. Local Israeli Monotype agents gathered information from current and potential clients and received various comments and requests for different Matrix Case Arrangements. However, Hebrew was considered a restricted market and new inquiries were met with hesitation. Eventually, Monotype decided not to cut new Hebrew typefaces due to the complex, time-consuming process and low profitability.[20]

Hebrew Monotype Typefaces at the Bixler Press and Letterfoundry

The Monotype Corporation played a central role in supporting Jewish printing, producing a relatively large number of Hebrew metal fonts over the years. While the Bixlers hold most of the Hebrew matrices, a focus was placed on the following three during the workshop: Peninim, Sonzino, and Schocken.

20
25
30
35
40

Peninim

The Peninim series 217, 220, and 489 was a version of the widely used Frank-Rühl typeface, created in Germany by Rafael Frank (1867–1920) and produced around 1910 by the C.F. Rühl Type Foundry. Eight years later, C.F. Rühl was acquired by the Berthold Type Foundry and the Frank-Rühl typeface appeared in their 1924 Hebrew specimen book. Around 1926, the Lerner & Teller company commissioned Monotype to produce a copy of Frank-Rühl. The typeface was released the following year under the name Peninim, which means "pearls" in Hebrew. Some modifications were introduced to the original design, such as lower contrast between horizontal and vertical strokes, distortion of numerous characters' proportions, and increased spacing between characters.[21]

א ב ג

ד ה ו ז

ח ט י כ ך

ל מ ם

נ ן ס ע

פ ף צ ץ

ק ר ש ת

24-point Peninim 220

Sonzino

The name of the Sonzino series 218 alludes to the fifteenth-century Soncino family of Italian Ashkenazi-Jewish printers, except it carries a German spelling. This typeface was initially released in 9-point size, concurrently with the production of the Peninim typeface.[22] Sonzino was the only Monotype typeface available with te'amim that were produced especially in addition to the niqqud.[23]

א

ב ג

ד ה ו

ז ח ט י

כ ך ל מ ם נ ן

ס ע פ ף

צ ץ ק

ר ש

ת

18-point Sonzino 218

Schocken

The Schocken series 547 and series 550 typefaces were initiated and drawn by the German-Israeli graphic designer and letterer Franzisca Esther Baruch (1901–1989). In 1936, in Mandatory Palestine, she was hired by Salman Schocken to redesign the layout, masthead, and logo for his Hebrew daily newspaper *Ha'aretz*, which means "the country" or "the land" in Hebrew. In 1937, Baruch presented him with her sketch of a Hebrew typeface she was developing at the time.

Schocken, and later on his son who inherited the newspaper and the press, were both dedicated to pursuing the creation of a new Hebrew typeface. In 1940, they commissioned Baruch to adapt her design for Monotype production in five sizes. In 1944, the Type Drawing Office at Monotype created matrix drawings that introduced many deviations from Baruch's original design. She did not approve the printing proofs when they arrived as the changes were still unsatisfactory and unacceptable. However, implementing Baruch's corrections required additional charges and production time was estimated at more than two years. Therefore, Schocken decided to carry on with the production and approve the matrices despite them being far from the original intent. In 1955, all five sizes of the Schocken typeface were ready for use in Ha'aretz Press Ltd. in Tel Aviv.[24] It was copyrighted to Ha'aretz for several years before it became available for public trade.[25]

א ב ג

ד ה ו ז ח

ט י כ ך ל

מ ם נ ן ס ע

פ ף צ ץ ק

ר ש ת

18-point Schocken 550

Bibliography

1 Ellen Leahy, “Making Books in Mottville,” *The Skaneateles Press of Skaneateles, New York* 173, no. 47 (November 2003): 1, 3.
2 Michael Bixler, “A Survey of American Typefounders,” *Bookways: A Quarterly for the Book* Arts, no. 7, (April 1993): 26.
3 Moshe Spitzer, *The Development of Hebrew lettering* (Jerusalem: Cultural and Scientific Relations Division, Ministry for Foreign Affairs, 1974), 10.
4 Raphael Posner and Israel Ta-Shema, eds. *The Hebrew book: an historical survey* (Jerusalem: Keter Publishing House, 1975), 86.
5 Nurit Pasternak, “Who Were the Hebrew Scribes in Renaissance Florence — A short review of their manifold roles,” *Bibliologia*, 38: *Manuscrits hébreux et arabes: Mélanges en l’honneur de Colette Sirat* (Turnhout: Brepols Publishers, 2014): 29–37.
6 Spitzer, 12, 18, 22.
7 Lanston Monotype, *The Monotype Specimen Book of Faces*, (Philadelphia, 1926), 3.
8 Jonathan D. Sarna, “Jewish Culture Comes to America,” *Jewish Studies* 42 (2003–2004): 45–57.
9 Lawrence W. Wallis, “Monotype Time Check,” in *One Hundred Years of Type-Making 1897–1997, Monotype Recorder*, New Series, no. 10 (1997): 48.
10 Cyrus Adler, “A New Hebrew Press,” *Journal of the American Oriental Society*, vol. 41 (1921): 225–229.
11 “A Revolution in the Composition of Hebrew,” *The Monotype Recorder*, vol. XXVI, no. 219 (1927): 12–17.
12 Johann Heinrich Gottfried Ernesti, *Die wol-eingerichtete Buchdruckerey* (Nürnberg: J.A. Endters seel Sohn und Erben, 1721), 50.
13 Cyrus, *A New Hebrew Press*, 225.
14 J. F. Coakley, *The Hebrew Types of the Jericho Press: A Specimen with Notes* (Ely, Jericho Press, 2010) 2.
15 “Voclized News”, *Davar newspaper*, 30 June, 1961, 3 [Hebrew].
16 Liron Lavi Turkenich, “From Frank Rühl to Peninim. A story of People, Type and Technology,” (MA diss. University of Reading, 2013), 23–31.

17 *A revolution in the composition of Hebrew*, 13–14.

18 Lavi Turkenich, 27.

19 Philipp Messner, "Schocken-Baruch: A New Hebrew Book Typeface," in *The Graphic Design of Moshe Spitzer, Franzisca Baruch, and Henri Friedlaender*, ed. Ada Wardi (Jerusalem: The Israel Museum, 2015–16), 239–253 [Hebrew edition].

20 Lavi Turkenich, 37, 77.

21 Lavi Turkenich, 31, 33.

22 Coakley, 8–9.

23 Lavi Turkenich, 49.

24 Philipp Messner, 241–252.

25 Lavi Turkenich, 67.

Appendix:
List of Known Hebrew Monotype Metal Typefaces

This list was compiled from the following available sources:

J. F. Coakley, *The Hebrew Types of the Jericho Press: A Specimen with Notes* (Ely, Jericho Press, 2010).

Liron Lavi Turkenich, "From Frank Rühl to Peninim. A story of People, Type and Technology" (MA diss. University of Reading, 2013).

"Monotype Metal Type Faces," The Alembic Press, accessed June 25, 2024, http://www.alembicpress.co.uk/Typecaster/numb.htm.

"Monotype Series Numbers," Effra Press & Typefoundry, accessed June 25, 2024, https://www.effrapress.co.uk/monotype-series-numbers/.

The Monotype Corporation Limited, *Specimen of 'Monotype' Non-Latin Faces* (London: 1977).

Lanston Monotype, *The Monotype Specimen Book of Faces,* (Philadelphia: 1926).

* The following series may have been produced for photo or digital composition in 1969: Alachsoni 733, Dak Jerushami 734, Ave Jerushami 735, Dak 736, Ave 737. In 1970, Deberny & Peignot's Koren typeface was produced as Koren book face 715 and Koren bold 716. Two more undated typefaces are noted as held in abeyance: Ave bold 998 and Alachsoni bold 999.

SERIES	NAME	POINT SIZE	YEARS	NOTES
280M	Classic Hebrew	4, 5, 6, 7, 8, 10	1926–n.d.	Produced by Lanston Monotype US
281M	Alperdob Hebrew	6, 8, 10	1926–n.d.	Produced by Lanston Monotype US
217	Peninim Pointed	6, 7, 7.5 partial, 8, 9 partial	1927–n.d.	Produced by C.F. Rühl, acquired by Berthold
218	Sonzino	9 with L41 niqqud, 12, 18	n.d.	
219	Ashurith	7, 8	n.d.	
220	Peninim	5, 6, 7, 14, 18, 24	n.d.	Produced by C.F. Rühl, acquired by Berthold
221	Levênim	7	1926–n.d.	Produced by C.F. Rühl, acquired by Berthold
222	Hebrew	6, 7, 8	1913–n.d.	
228	Rabbinic	11, 12	1927–n.d.	
487	Gill	12	n.d.–1967	
488	Mayer	Unknown	n.d.	
489	Peninim Reversed	8, 7 partial	1937–n.d.	For casting with Latin
492	Mayer	10	n.d.	
547	Schocken No. 1	6, 7, 9	1947–1974	Proprietary
550	Schocken No. 2	14, 18	1947–1967	Proprietary
551	Schocken No. 3	Unknown	n.d.–1967	Proprietary

About the Author

Shani Avni is the Ismar David Visiting Assistant Curator at the RIT Cary Graphic Arts Collection since 2020. She holds a BA in Graphic Design from Shenkar College Israel, and an MA in Typeface Design from the University of Reading, United Kingdom. For her thesis she researched the David Hebrew typeface family and, since receiving her degree, continues to do so. She designs, researches, teaches, consults, writes, and lectures on Jewish type and typography. She perseveres in her efforts to strengthen the connection between the academic and practical spheres through the accessibility of historical information.

Colophon

This chapbook was produced in 2024 to document the Hebrew Type Intensive workshop held at the Press and Letterfoundry of Michael and Winifred Bixler in July 2023.
Cover and type specimens letterpress-printed by Richard Kegler at Dry Inc. with the assistance of Javier Viramontes. Text, images, and design by Shani Avni.
The featured typeface is Maiola by Veronika Burian. Hebrew Type Intensive portfolio photographs by R.H. Hensleigh. Printed digitally with HP Indigo on Mohawk Superfine. Produced with the support of the Gladys Krieble Delmas Foundation, the American Printing History Association (APHA), and the APHA Upstate New York Chapter.
Special thanks to Helen Brandshaft, James Coakley, Amelia Hugill-Fontanel, David McNamara, Noam Sienna, and Liron Lavi Turkenich.

Printed in an edition of 200 copies.
This is # 192